Creatures All Around Us

Frogs, Frogs Everywhere

 Carolrhoda Books, Inc./Minneapolis

The publisher wishes to thank James Gerholdt, The Remarkable Reptiles, for his help in the preparation of this book.

Carolrhoda Books, Inc. c/o The Lerner Group
241 First Avenue North, Minneapolis, MN 55401

Library of Congress Cataloging-in-Publication Data
Souza, D. M. (Dorothy M.)
    Frogs, frogs everywhere / by D. M. Souza
        p.   cm. — (Creatures all around us)
    Includes index.
    ISBN 0-87614-825-9
    1. Frogs—Juvenile literature. [1. Frogs.] I. Title. II. Series:
Souza, D. M. (Dorothy M.). Creatures all around us.
    QL668.E2S738   1994
    597.8—dc20   94-6897
                                                          CIP
                                                          AC

Manufactured in the United States of America
1 2 3 4 5 6 I/JR 00 99 98 97 96 95

A Northern red-legged frog

Frogs, Frogs Everywhere

A chorus of croaking, honking, peeping sounds fills the night air. It is coming from hundreds of different frogs and toads. Some are floating between reeds in a pond or are perched on lily pads. Others are peeking out from under fallen logs. A few are hopping off the leaves or branches of trees and shrubs.

3

Most of the creatures are green, gray, brown, or spotted green and brown. One could fit on the end of your finger. Another is bigger than your hand. All of these frogs and toads are members of a large group of animals known as **amphibians** (am-FIB-ee-unz). The group also includes salamanders and long, legless animals known as caecilians (sih-SIL-yunz). Caecilians live underground in hot climates.

The word *amphibian* comes from two Greek words meaning "double life." The term describes creatures that can live both on land and in water. In the first part of their lives, the **larval** stage, many amphibians live like fish in water. In another part, the adult stage, some crawl, hop, or jump around on land most of the time, while others remain in the water all the time.

No matter where they are, all amphibians must have water or moist sand or soil. They need moisture to keep their skins from drying out. While their glands produce mucus, making a number of amphibians look and feel slimy, this does not totally protect them from dry, hot air. In summer, those that live away from water must bury themselves in moist places under logs, rocks, or soil. Only when the air turns cool at night can they safely come out to hunt.

An Eastern spadefoot toad at its burrow. Spadefoot toads use their hind feet to dig burrows where they can keep cool on hot days.

A green frog taking in water in a pond

Many adult amphibians breathe by means of lungs, just as humans and other mammals do, but they also take in air through their thin skins and the wet linings of their mouths. Tiny blood vessels close to the surface of the skin pick up needed oxygen from the air and water and carry it through the amphibians' bodies.

The creatures take in water in much the same way. You won't see an amphibian lapping up a drink the way your dog or cat does. It will simply sit in a pool of water and soak it up as if it were a kitchen sponge.

Like fish and reptiles, amphibians are cold-blooded, or **ectothermic** (ek-tuh-THUR-mik). This does not mean that their blood is cold, but rather that their body temperatures change with the temperature of their surroundings. When it's too hot or too cold outside, the animals must hide to protect themselves. Different kinds of frogs, as we shall see, have special hiding places.

Of the more than 4,000 species, or kinds, of amphibians that have been discovered, frogs and toads are the most numerous. More than 3,500 varieties can be found in ponds, streams, woods, and caves around the world. Many live in hot climates, and a few even survive in the Arctic Circle. Let's find out how some of them live.

Family Matters

A male green frog, a member of the true frog family

Sitting in the shade of a shrub is a greenish brown frog about 5 inches long. It has smooth skin, big bulging eyes near the top of its head, and long hind legs. It is a green frog—a member of the family of true frogs. Leopard frogs, bullfrogs, and wood frogs, among others, also belong to this family.

10

Close by is a slightly smaller creature. It has rough, brownish skin with wartlike bumps, a bulge on each side of its neck, and hind legs shorter than the frog's. It is an American toad—a member of the family of true toads.

Many creatures have the word *frog* or *toad* in their names. But this does not always mean that they are members of the true frog or true toad family. It simply means that some are more like true frogs, while others are more like true toads.

There are about twenty related families of frogs and toads living around the world. Eight of them are found in North America. Scientists call all the members of these families *anurans* (uh-NYUR-unz), a word meaning "tailless." But many scientists use the word *frog* when speaking of any anuran, whether it is froglike or toadlike.

An American toad. Note its bumpy skin.

The green frog we spotted sitting in the shade spends its time both in and out of the water. Powerful muscles in its long hind legs help it shoot through the air like a rocket. Its relative, the leopard frog, may leap 5 feet. That's 12 times the length of its own body.

The green frog is also an expert swimmer. If you can do the "frog kick," you know how it moves through the water. By bringing its hind legs and webbed feet close to its body and pushing back against the water, it zooms ahead.

A Northern leopard frog shows its swimming skills.

An American toad burrowing into the soft earth at the base of a tree

The true toad, sitting close by, looks similar to the frog but is less streamlined. It does not leap, but only hops. Its warty skin holds moisture better than the frog's and does not dry out as fast. For this reason, the toad can and does live farther from water than most frogs.

During the day it hides in burrows that have been abandoned by other animals. Frequently it digs a hideout of its own. The warty bumps on its back and the bulges, called **parotoid** (PAR-uh-toyd) **glands,** on either side of its neck, contain a thick, white poison that can paralyze or kill some enemies if they try to eat the toad.

Vividly colored poison-arrow frogs like the ones shown here are found in Central and South America.

Other families of anurans aren't exactly like true frogs or true toads. Members of the family of poison-arrow frogs are brilliantly colored. Surinam toads of South America and African clawed toads never leave the water, while tree frogs spend their time clinging to the leaves and branches of trees. Some can even change colors. Spadefoot toads are able to live in the hottest, driest deserts of the world.

Actually, if all the families of anurans paraded in front of you, you might not believe they were all related to each other.

Singing in the Pond

*A male bullfrog in the pond where
he will find a mate*

A male bullfrog about as wide as a grapefruit is sitting in the water. He is green with brown patches on his back. Beneath his large head is a loose sac of yellow skin. He takes a deep gulp of air, then, a few minutes later, a booming "jug-o-rum" echoes across the pond. With this call, he is inviting a female bullfrog into his territory.

A variety of other male frogs and toads are sending out different calls in and around the pond. They are doing it by pumping air back and forth over their vocal cords. Some, including the bullfrog, have vocal sacs under their chins that balloon out and make their calls sound even louder.

Jingling bells, peeping birds, whistles, snores, grunts, and barks are just a few of the things anurans' calls sound like. And the largest creatures do not always make the loudest noises. Spring peepers, which are only about an inch long, can be heard a half-mile away.

Each frog's call lets females of the same species know where to find a mate. Females do not answer mating calls, although they do sometimes make sounds when they're in trouble.

This male spring peeper's vocal sac inflates as he makes his call.

An Eastern wood frog holds his mate in amplexus.

After hearing a few more "jug-o-rums," one female bullfrog enters the water and swims toward the big male. He grabs her from behind with his front legs, piggyback style, and gives her a sort of hug. This position is called **amplexus** (am-PLEK-sus). While in this position, the pair dives just below the surface of the water, and the female begins laying her eggs. The male sprays the eggs with **sperm,** or male cells, which **fertilize** (FUR-tul-eyz) them, or help them begin to develop.

Other kinds of anurans meet, dance, swim around, or go through mock fights before they mate. But most of the males hold the females in the same way, from behind, either under her front legs or close to her hind ones.

During this time of year, males of a number of species develop spiny growths on their fingers. The growths are known as nuptial pads, and they help the males grasp females in the water.

The female may begin to lay eggs for the male to fertilize very soon after the two anurans get together, or she may not do so for several hours. The number of eggs a female lays varies, depending on her size and species. The female bullfrog lays as many as five thousand eggs, while the much smaller spring peeper lays about eight hundred. Other species lay as few as two.

This female Pacific chorus frog has laid her eggs, and now her mate will fertilize them.

A clump of wood frog eggs attached to a plant in a pond

The tiny eggs do not have shells the way birds' eggs do. Instead, a jellylike covering surrounds them and holds them together in clumps or long strings. Masses of eggs float on the surface of the water or are attached to rocks and plant stems in the water. Leeches, fish, insects, birds, and snapping turtles prowl the water, waiting to snatch a mouthful whenever they can.

Usually, after females have released their eggs, they leave the pond. Males swim away and begin calling for other mates. Not all frogs leave their eggs unprotected, however. Males of some American chorus frog species watch over the eggs. Female Surinam toads and some tree frogs of Central and South America carry their eggs around on their backs. Females of a few species even carry their eggs inside their bodies until they are fully developed. Then miniature adults slip out of the females' cloacas (klo-EH-kuhz), openings at the back of their bodies.

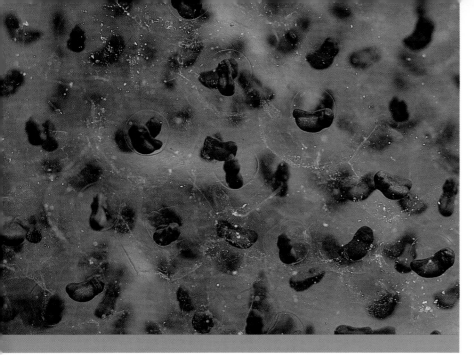

Tadpoles

You can clearly see the developing embryos in these wood frog eggs.

Within an hour after they have been fertilized, the eggs begin changing. Slowly each **embryo** (EM-bree-oh), or developing creature, twists and turns inside its transparent case. Bumps and pockets appear until finally a head, body, and tail take shape.

Some anurans, such as spadefoot toads, hatch in as little as two days. Others, such as bullfrogs, may take two weeks. If the weather is especially warm or cold, hatching times may change.

A recently hatched wood frog tadpole

Most newly hatched anurans are known as tadpoles, and they must have water in order to survive. At first, they hang by their sticky heads from their cases or from surrounding plants. Then they begin swimming. Many look very much like fish. They have lidless eyes, finlike tails, and thin skin. Most are strong swimmers and wiggle around, feeding almost continuously on algae and other pond plants. They scrape their food off rocks and logs with their rows of rough-edged teeth and with the sharp edges of their jaws. Some tadpoles, such as those of American bell toads, have suckers on their mouths. These help them hold onto rocks in fast-moving streams.

A growing bullfrog tadpole. By the time most tadpoles are a few weeks old, a layer of skin has grown over their gills.

Like fish, tadpoles breathe through **gills,** feathery structures on the sides of their heads. After water enters their mouths, it passes across the gills. Air is sifted out, and the water leaves through an opening called a **spiracle** (SPIR-uh-kul) that is usually on the left side of the head.

As the tadpoles grow, they may double or triple in size in a few days or weeks. Their heads widen, and their eyes become larger and move toward the tops of their heads. Tadpoles that hatch in rain puddles or ditches, as some toads do, must do all of this quickly, before the water around them dries out.

This bullfrog tadpole is beginning metamorphosis. Notice the hind leg that has formed near the base of its tail.

Some true frog tadpoles spend their first winter buried in the mud at the bottom of the pond. But, like most of their relatives, they eventually go through some startling changes that turn them into frogs. This process is known as **metamorphosis** (met-uh-MOR-fuh-sis).

First two small bumps appear along the sides of the tail. Then hind legs break through the skin there. Eyes become larger, and lungs begin to develop inside the body. Later, the frogs will breathe through these lungs instead of through their gills, which will disappear.

In a few weeks, front legs appear, one at a time. Mouths widen as tongues develop and jaws become stronger. Skin grows thicker, nostrils appear, and tails shorten until they finally disappear.

The young frogs can now hop onto the bank, hide between blades of grass, or leap back into the water. They spend most of their time catching insects or escaping the predators that enjoy snacking on them.

This young leopard frog has almost completed metamorphosis, but you can still see the stub of its tail.

Frogs through the Year

An Eastern wood frog prepares to catch and eat an aphid.

Flies are buzzing in and around the branches of a sweet-smelling bush. A young, olive gray tree frog, smaller than a paper clip, crawls up a branch. Like other tree frogs, it has sticky pads on each of its toes and fingers to keep it from falling. It climbs closer to one fly and—zap! It catches a meal.

Near a roadside pond, several mosquitoes are humming above the water. A southern toad sits close by. It watches with bulging eyes as one mosquito flies near. Zap! It catches and swallows the tiny insect.

Anurans spend much of their time eating. During their lives they catch millions of insects, their favorite food.

Some also eat earthworms, slugs, shrimps, mollusks, and small fish. What they eat depends not only on their size, but also on the food that is available where they live. Narrow-mouthed frogs, which hide under rocks and logs, eat mostly ants. Toads that inhabit dry places eat many millipedes, ants, spiders, and beetles. Mink frogs, which live in bogs, catch live water creatures. A few frogs in hot climates even swallow mice, rats, and lizards whole.

A pickerel frog making a meal of a worm

Some frogs even eat other frogs. You can see the foot of a smaller frog sticking out of this red-legged frog's mouth.

Tongues play an especially important part in helping frogs catch a meal. Their tongues are rooted in the front of their mouths and can dart in and out faster than you can blink an eye. With their sticky surfaces, they grab onto an insect. If it's too big, the anuran stuffs it into its mouth with its front fingers. If the insect tries to escape, teeth in the frog's upper jaw hold it in place.

A Southern toad leaving its burrow

When the weather turns cold, the frog's body also becomes cold. To keep from freezing to death, the animal **hibernates** (HY-bur-nayts)—it goes into a sleeplike state in a hiding place. Green frogs crawl into a bed of mud under water to hibernate. Bullfrogs swim to the bottom of a pond. Spring peepers snuggle under leaves, and many toads dig holes underground. Hundreds of frogs may hibernate together.

Once in hiding, all stop eating. Heartbeats slow, and so does the flow of blood. Many breathe through their skins instead of through their lungs.

Not until the temperatures warm do the hibernating frogs "come alive" again and begin hopping and leaping around in search of insects. They must constantly be on the lookout for the birds, fish, reptiles, mammals, and other amphibians that like to catch and eat them.

28

The large circle below this green frog's eye is a tympanic membrane.

Watch Out!

A hawk swoops close to the ground and swishes through the air. A frog hears it with two circles of skin on either side of its head. These patches of skin are called **tympanic** (tim-PAN-ik) **membranes,** or tympanums (TIM-pun-umz).

If an enemy makes a sound, the membranes vibrate. The vibration travels to the frog's inner ear and sends a signal to its brain that danger is near.

In an instant, the creature leaps into the pond and dives to the bottom. Each of its eyes has a top and bottom lid. Beneath the bottom one is a thin, clear covering called the **nictitating** (NIK-tih-tayt-ing) **membrane.** As the frog dives, this third lid closes and acts like a pair of swimming goggles, protecting the frog's eyes.

After about fifteen minutes at the bottom of the pond, the frog swims to the surface again. But this time only its bulging eyes poke out above the water. When it discovers that the hawk has disappeared, it leaps back onto the bank.

Frogs have a number of ways of escaping predators, but hopping or leaping to safety is one of the best. Another is to **camouflage** (KAM-uh-flazh) themselves, or change their skin color to blend in with their surroundings.

The canyon tree frog, when frightened, frequently changes from dark brownish gray to nearly black. Other tree frogs change from green to brown and back to green again, depending upon the light or the temperature.

Both of the frogs below are canyon tree frogs. They can change color to blend in with the landscape around them.

This barking frog has puffed itself up to make it harder for an enemy to swallow it.

Some anurans escape danger by playing dead. If threatened, the gopher frog of Florida goes into a trance. After a while, it scoots a few steps away from its predator and plays dead again. It does the same thing until it is two or three feet away from its would-be attacker. Then it jumps out of sight.

Cricket frogs often play dead in the water. They float around like leaves. Their arms and legs become stiff and they stop taking in air through their lungs.

Many frogs are able to puff themselves up until they are too big for a predator to swallow. The barking frog of the southwestern United States, for example, lives in holes and rock crevices. To keep predators from pulling it out of its hideout, it swells up to an enormous size.

When alarmed, most toads can release poison from their warts and parotoid glands. A dog or other predator that grabs a toad quickly learns never to do it again. The milky poison floods the predator's mouth, burning the tender lining and sometimes making the animal deathly sick. Some toads, including the Colorado River toad and the marine toad, are more poisonous than others.

Most toads produce poison, and a few frogs do it too. The most deadly ones, the poison-arrow frogs, live in Central and South America. They are only ½ to 1½ inches long and are brilliantly colored, probably to warn away enemies. Native people in the jungles have for centuries used the frogs' poisons on the tips of arrows and blow darts. When these weapons strike, they can cause paralysis and death.

While most frogs in the wild probably do not survive more than a few years, some in captivity may outlive their enemies. One bullfrog hopped in and out of a backyard pond for ten years, and a European toad lived in a family's garden for thirty-six years. How many insects do you think they ate during their lives?

Above: *The marine toad's poison is strong enough to kill an animal.* Below: *Poison-arrow frogs are beautiful but dangerous.*

Disappearing

An arroyo toad

Before 1930, tens of thousands of plump little arroyo toads hid in the forests of coastal Southern California. They lived nowhere else in the world.

Then, gradually, homes and highways began dotting and crossing their **habitats,** the places where they lived. With fewer places for them to hide, arroyo toads began disappearing.

The Pine Barrens tree frog, found in the northeastern United States, is now rare because much of the area where it once lived has been taken over by roads and buildings.

Between 1987 and 1993, little rain fell in California, and ponds and streams dried up. With no water, the toads could not mate, and females could not lay their eggs. With no new tadpoles to take the place of older toads, scientists worried that arroyo toads would become **extinct,** or die off until none are left.

What happened to this little toad is also happening to many other amphibians around the world. As forests, meadows, and waterways are replaced by homes, offices, and freeways, the creatures have fewer places to hide. Without ponds or streams in which to mate, they cannot survive or create new members of their species. Those that crowd into remaining waterways are frequently threatened by pesticides and other dangerous chemicals that destroy thousands of their fragile eggs and developing young.

The Puerto Rican toad at right and the Amaragosa River toad on the next page, like many kinds of frogs and toads around the world, are in danger of becoming extinct.

The more we learn about these lively creatures, the more
we can do to help protect them and their habitats. Then for
many years to come everyone will be able to enjoy watching
them and listening to their many peeps, squeaks, grunts,
and jug-o-rum sounds.

Scientists who study animals group them together according to their similarities and differences. These groups are given names in Latin. Animals that have certain features in common are placed in the same order. All frogs belong to the order Anura. Within this order, there are many different families. Below are some of the members of four well-known families of frogs, along with a few facts about them. All of these frogs can be found in North America.

FAMILY	EXAMPLES	LONGEST IN INCHES	MATING CALL	HABITAT
Bufonidae	American toad	5	musical trill	gardens, fields, wooded areas
	Oak toad	$1\frac{1}{4}$	high-pitched peep	ditches, ponds, pools
	Southern toad	$3\frac{7}{8}$	high trill	loose soil
Ranidae	Bullfrog	8	"jug-o-rum"	marshes, ponds, lakes, rivers
	Green frog	4	"tung"	swamps, brooks, streams
	Northern leopard frog	5	low trill	streams, swamps, marshes
	Wood frog	$3\frac{1}{4}$	sharp clacking	woods close to ponds, swamps
Hylidae	Spring peeper	$1\frac{3}{8}$	high, whistling peep	marshes, ponds, wooded areas
	Green tree frog	$2\frac{1}{2}$	"quonk" or "quank"	pools, edges of waterways
	Little grass frog	$\frac{3}{4}$	high tinkling	moist areas around ponds
Pelobatidae	Eastern spadefoot	$2\frac{7}{8}$	"ker-r-aw"	sandy soil in forests
	Plains spadefoot	$2\frac{1}{2}$	a squawk	sandy soil in prairies
	Western spadefoot	$2\frac{1}{2}$	a snort	streams and temporary ponds

Glossary

amphibians: a class of animals that are able to live both on land and in water

amplexus: the position in which male frogs hold female frogs during mating

camouflage: to blend in with the surroundings

ectothermic: having a body temperature that changes depending on the temperature of the environment

embryo: the young of an animal in the beginning stages of development

extinct: having no members of a species left alive

fertilization: the process of a sperm and an egg joining to form a new individual

gills: organs that some animals use for breathing

habitats: places where a particular type of animal lives

hibernate: to spend the winter in a hiding place, in a sleeplike state

larval: the first life stage of some animals, including amphibians

metamorphosis: a series of changes in which a larval animal becomes an adult

nictitating membrane: a thin layer that covers a frog's eye and protects it when the frog is underwater

parotoid glands: structures on a frog's body that contain poison

sperm: the male cells that fertilize a female's eggs

spiracle: an opening on the side of a frog's head through which water leaves its body

tympanic membranes: the structures on a frog's head with which it senses sounds

Index

The photographs are reproduced through the courtesy of: © Dr. Alan K. Mallams, front cover, p. 35; © Breck P. Kent, back cover, pp. 3, 10, 14 (right), 15, 19, 20, 21, 23, 33 (bottom); © Jack Dermid, pp. 5, 11; © Rob Simpson, pp. 6, 33 (top); © John Serrao, pp. 7, 26; © Michael P. Turco, p. 9; © Dan Nedrelo, p. 12; © Nick Bergkessel, pp. 13, 16, 17, 25; © Allen Blake Sheldon, pp. 14 (left), 22; © 1994 Klaus O. Richter, pp. 18, 29; © J.H. Robinson, pp. 24, 28; © Anthony Mercieca/Root Resources, p. 27; © Fred Whitehead, p. 30; © David Liebman, p. 31; © Manny Rubio, pp. 34, 36, 37.